An Analysis of

Robert A. Dahl's

Who Governs?
Democracy and Power in an American City

Astrid Noren Nilsson
with
Jason Xidias

Copyright © 2017 by Macat International Ltd
24:13 Coda Centre, 189 Munster Road, London SW6 6AW.

Macat International has asserted its right under the Copyright, Designs and Patents Act
1988 to be identified as the copyright holder of this work.

www.macat.com
info@macat.com

Cover illustration: Etienne Gilfillan

Cataloguing in Publication Data
A catalogue record for this book is available from the British Library.
Library of Congress Cataloguing-in-Publication Data is available upon request.

ISBN 978-1-912303-23-6 (hardback)
ISBN 978-1-912128-00-6 (paperback)
ISBN 978-1-912282-11-1 (e-book)

Notice

CONTENTS

WAYS IN TO THE TEXT

Who Was Robert A. Dahl?   9
What Does *Who Governs?* Say?   10
Why Does *Who Governs?* Matter?   12

SECTION 1: INFLUENCES

Module 1: The Author and the Historical Context   15
Module 2: Academic Context   19
Module 3: The Problem   23
Module 4: The Author's Contribution   27

SECTION 2: IDEAS

Module 5: Main Ideas   32
Module 6: Secondary Ideas   35
Module 7: Achievement   38
Module 8: Place in the Author's Work   42

SECTION 3: IMPACT

Module 9: The First Responses   47
Module 10: The Evolving Debate   51
Module 11: Impact and Influence Today   55
Module 12: Where Next?   59

Glossary of Terms   63
People Mentioned in the Text   66
Works Cited   72

THE MACAT LIBRARY
The Macat Library is a series of unique academic explorations of seminal works in the humanities and social sciences – books and papers that have had a significant and widely recognised impact on their disciplines. It has been created to serve as much more than just a summary of what lies between the covers of a great book. It illuminates and explores the influences on, ideas of, and impact of that book. Our goal is to offer a learning resource that encourages critical thinking and fosters a better, deeper understanding of important ideas.

Each publication is divided into three Sections: Influences, Ideas, and Impact. Each Section has four Modules. These explore every important facet of the work, and the responses to it.

This Section-Module structure makes a Macat Library book easy to use, but it has another important feature. Because each Macat book is written to the same format, it is possible (and encouraged!) to cross-reference multiple Macat books along the same lines of inquiry or research. This allows the reader to open up interesting interdisciplinary pathways.

To further aid your reading, lists of glossary terms and people mentioned are included at the end of this book (these are indicated by an asterisk [*] throughout) – as well as a list of works cited.

Macat has worked with the University of Cambridge to identify the elements of critical thinking and understand the ways in which six different skills combine to enable effective thinking.
Three allow us to fully understand a problem; three more give us the tools to solve it. Together, these six skills make up the **PACIER** model of critical thinking. They are:

ANALYSIS – understanding how an argument is built
EVALUATION – exploring the strengths and weaknesses of an argument
INTERPRETATION – understanding issues of meaning

CREATIVE THINKING – coming up with new ideas and fresh connections
PROBLEM-SOLVING – producing strong solutions
REASONING – creating strong arguments

To find out more, visit **WWW.MACAT.COM.**

CRITICAL THINKING AND *WHO GOVERNS?*

Primary critical thinking skill: CREATIVE THINKING
Secondary critical thinking skill: ANALYSIS

American political theorist Robert Dahl's 1961 work of political theory exhibits deep levels of creative thinking. When Dahl wrote, the American system of liberal democracy was generally considered to be shaped by a small group of powerful individuals who dominate because they are wealthy and influential. But by connecting the evidence in a new way in *Who Governs?* Dahl argued convincingly against this view.

Dahl suggested that power is actually distributed among a number of competing groups, and that each of those groups seeks to influence decisions. He puts forward a definition of political power as the ability to make others do what you want them to, concluding that – while most people do not actively participate in politics and so do not exert a direct influence – power is still fragmented, and citizens do indirectly shape decision-making.

Dahl's novel explanation of the existing evidence emerged from a study of three areas of policy-making in the city of New Haven: political nominations, urban redevelopment, and public education. His research revealed that different people wielded power in each area, and that only the mayor, whose power is checked by those who vote for him, was powerful in all three. These new connections allowed Dahl to arrive at fresh conclusions and convincingly demonstrated that the US operates a pluralist system in which power is divided between different interest groups.

ABOUT THE AUTHOR OF THE ORIGINAL WORK

Robert A. Dahl was born in 1915 in Iowa in the United States. He received his PhD in political science from Yale University in 1940, and after serving in the US Army during World War II, returned to Yale to become a professor, spending his entire academic career there. Over the next 40 years, Dahl wrote prolifically and many of his works, including *Who Governs? Democracy and Power in an American City* (1961), became key texts in the field of political science. Dahl also won a number of prestigious awards and helped Yale's department of political science become one of the most respected in the country. He died in 2014 at the age of 98.

ABOUT THE AUTHORS OF THE ANALYSIS

Dr Astrid Noren Nilsson holds a doctorate in politics and international studies from the University of Cambridge. She currently teaches at the University of Lund in Sweden, and is the author of the monograph *Cambodia's Second Kingdom: Nation, Imagination, and Democracy* (Cornell SEAP, 2016). Her research interests include democratic change, nationalism, the politics of memory, and emerging notions of citizenship and social change in South-East Asia.

Dr Jason Xidias holds a PhD in European Politics from King's College London, where he completed a comparative dissertation on immigration and citizenship in Britain and France. He was also a Visiting Fellow in European Politics at the University of California, Berkeley. Currently, he is Lecturer in Political Science at New York University.

ABOUT MACAT

GREAT WORKS FOR CRITICAL THINKING

Macat is focused on making the ideas of the world's great thinkers accessible and comprehensible to everybody, everywhere, in ways that promote the development of enhanced critical thinking skills.

It works with leading academics from the world's top universities to produce new analyses that focus on the ideas and the impact of the most influential works ever written across a wide variety of academic disciplines. Each of the works that sit at the heart of its growing library is an enduring example of great thinking. But by setting them in context – and looking at the influences that shaped their authors, as well as the responses they provoked – Macat encourages readers to look at these classics and game-changers with fresh eyes. Readers learn to think, engage and challenge their ideas, rather than simply accepting them.

'Macat offers an amazing first-of-its-kind tool for interdisciplinary learning and research. Its focus on works that transformed their disciplines and its rigorous approach, drawing on the world's leading experts and educational institutions, opens up a world-class education to anyone.'

Andreas Schleicher
Director for Education and Skills, Organisation for Economic Co-operation and Development

'Macat is taking on some of the major challenges in university education ... They have drawn together a strong team of active academics who are producing teaching materials that are novel in the breadth of their approach.'

Prof Lord Broers,
former Vice-Chancellor of the University of Cambridge

'The Macat vision is exceptionally exciting. It focuses upon new modes of learning which analyse and explain seminal texts which have profoundly influenced world thinking and so social and economic development. It promotes the kind of critical thinking which is essential for any society and economy.
This is the learning of the future.'

Rt Hon Charles Clarke, former UK Secretary of State for Education

'The Macat analyses provide immediate access to the critical conversation surrounding the books that have shaped their respective discipline, which will make them an invaluable resource to all of those, students and teachers, working in the field.'

Professor William Tronzo, University of California at San Diego

WAYS IN TO THE TEXT

KEY POINTS

- Robert A. Dahl's book *Who Governs?* was part of the behavioralist* revolution of the 1950s and 1960s in the United States—a movement in the field of political science that stressed that findings and arguments should be based on evidence that could be verified by observation.

- In *Who Governs?*, Dahl studies power and influence in the city of New Haven, Connecticut, which he argued was a microcosm (a representation in miniature) of American democracy.

- Dahl concluded that policy-making in America was shaped by competing interest groups (the "pluralist"* argument) rather than by a small group of powerful individuals (the "elitist"* argument), as was generally believed. On publication, pluralist theory became the dominant perspective on American democracy.

Who Was Robert A. Dahl?

Robert A. Dahl (1915–2014), the author of *Who Governs? Democracy and Power in an American City*, was one of the great political scientists of the twentieth century. Over more than 60 years, he transformed our understanding of democracy by publishing two dozen books and hundreds of journal articles.

Dahl grew up in the US states of Iowa and Alaska. After graduating from the University of Washington in 1936, he pursued his doctorate in political science at Yale University. During World War II,* Dahl served in the US Army and was awarded the distinguished Bronze Star Medal. Dahl joined the faculty at Yale University in 1946, where he was to spend his entire academic career. He played a fundamental role in positioning Yale's political science department as one of the best in the world. As professor, and later professor emeritus, Dahl championed democracy both in theory and practice.

While Dahl published several important texts, his best known is *Who Governs?* (1961), a case study of how power and influence operate in New Haven, Connecticut. Dahl argues that although American democracy has many shortcomings, including a significant gap between rich and poor, it is nevertheless exemplary in many ways—an argument similar to that made over a hundred years earlier by the French political theorist Alexis de Tocqueville* in his 1835 work *Democracy in America*.

In later texts, such as *Democracy and its Critics* (1989), Dahl became far more critical of democracy, pointing to rising inequalities in the world's most developed nations and questioning whether any government should be called democratic.

What Does *Who Governs?* Say?

In *Who Governs?*, Dahl studies three areas of policy-making in the city of New Haven: political nominations, urban redevelopment, and public education. He finds that different people wield power in each area, with only the mayor, whose power is checked by those who vote for him, powerful in all three. His conclusion is that New Haven is a *pluralist* system—a system in which power is divided between different interest groups.

Dahl argues that power is not a physical substance possessed in fixed amounts; it is something that stems from certain kinds of resources used to influence others to behave in certain ways. Dahl argues that almost no one is free from sources of influence. Though many people do not vote or participate directly in politics, they still contribute to public opinion, which influences policy-making.

Different political resources,* Dahl argues, such as wealth and social status, affect different policy areas; no single resource determines all or even most decisions. Additionally, resources themselves are only potential power. They must be mobilized by political actors—e.g., politicians, bureaucrats, and lobbyists—in order to influence decisions; wealth, for example, only confers power if people can use money to influence others.

In New Haven, Dahl found that the local upper-class was not based in the business community, as some political scientists had previously suggested. The business community sometimes blocked policies it disagreed with, but it did not play an active role in influencing decision-making. Interestingly, Dahl observed that Yale University had only minimal influence on local politics.

While there were inequalities in the city, they were not concentrated in any particular segment of the population. Instead, power was dispersed, with no one group completely blocked off from political participation. In short, the system was relatively meritocratic*—that is, people with influence had been selected according to their capacity to exercise that influence successfully. Furthermore, politicians believed that responding to citizens' demands would help them win elections. Dahl demonstrated this arrangement of dispersed inequalities, openness to political participation, and fragmented power with significant empirical* data—that is, evidence verifiable by observation. In so doing, he positioned pluralism as the dominant perspective on democracy in political science.

Dahl's conclusion contradicts the claims of the activist and scholar Floyd Hunter* and the sociologist C. Wright Mills,* both of whom believed that a small group of powerful ("elite") individuals shaped policy-making. This theory is known as elitism.* Hunter reached this conclusion based on his study of Atlanta, Georgia, and Mills after analyzing the relationship between political, economic, and military elites at a national level in the United States.

Why Does *Who Governs?* Matter?

As a successful challenge to elite theory, then the dominant perspective on American democracy, *Who Governs?* deeply affected the field of political science.

Dahl conducted a case study of power and influence in the city of New Haven believing that the local political structure resembled that of the nation's federal system; one of America's older cities, it featured a strong two-party* political system. In practice, the author found that competing interest groups, rather than a powerful group of individuals, shaped local politics and decision-making. Dahl then applied this finding more broadly at a national level, concluding that the United States was a pluralist democracy—that is, one characterized by competing interest groups and a fragmentation of power.

Dahl's study was based on two years of data collection and analysis, including interviews with key figures in the city. It was an important contribution to the behavioralist revolution of the 1950s and 1960s, a turn in the field of political science towards scientifically tested evidence. Previously, political scholars had drawn on political philosophy to make predictions about the future; these predictions were based on what were perceived as "normal" patterns of behavior, and were not always grounded in fieldwork. Dahl believed that this was far too simplistic, and that the social sciences should approach their work the same way as the natural sciences.

Today, Robert A. Dahl is widely recognized as one of history's great political scientists, and his work serves as a foundation for examining democracy both in the United States and around the world. Dahl's understanding of power, and how competing actors shape power, remain seminal concepts, while his later texts address other areas, including citizenship, foreign policy, welfare policy, the US Constitution,* and the US Congress* (both key parts of the legal and governmental structures of the United States). In these later works, Dahl reflects deeply on economic and political inequalities in modern democracies and questions the extent to which the United States and other nations are truly democratic. He also analyzes the US Constitution in detail and considers how it could be updated to improve society.

Taken as a whole, Dahl's work offers an increasingly sophisticated understanding of how democracy functions.

SECTION 1
INFLUENCES

MODULE 1
THE AUTHOR AND THE
HISTORICAL CONTEXT

KEY POINTS

- Robert A. Dahl published *Who Governs?* in 1961 in response to a debate between pluralist* and elitist* theorists. Though Dahl was a pluralist, he believed that neither side had enough empirical* evidence for their claims.

- Upon publication, Dahl's pluralist view replaced elite theory as the leading perspective on democracy in America and elsewhere. Today, neo-pluralism,* a modernized version of Dahl's original argument, is most dominant.

- Dahl's extensive training in political science and his passion for understanding how democracy worked shaped *Who Governs?*

Why Read This Text?

Robert A. Dahl's *Who Governs? Democracy and Power in an American City* was a game-changer when it was published in 1961 because it established pluralism, the theory that power is distributed between multiple groups, as the dominant perspective on American democracy. The book remains influential today and is commonly taught in political science courses.

Who Governs? was inspired in part by an important debate during the 1950s and 1960s between elitist and pluralist theorists over what constituted power and influence in American democracy. Dahl challenged elitist political theory, then the leading perspective, according to which power was concentrated among a few powerful people, by showing that elitist thought could not account for the

> **❝** When Bob Dahl became a leading figure in political science, the Yale political science department was, in large part because of his presence, by far and away the best political science department in the country. **❞**
>
> Jacob Hacker, *Yale Daily News,* February 7, 2014

complexities of politics and decision-making. He also criticized previous pluralist thinkers, such as the political scientists Arthur F. Bentley* and David Truman,* for not presenting adequate empirical evidence to support their claims. Dahl spent two years conducting interviews and collecting data in New Haven, Connecticut. He concluded that multiple competing actors, such as politicians, bureaucrats, and lobbyists, shaped politics at both the municipal and national levels in the United States.

Today, the leading view on American democracy is neo-pluralism, a modified and modernized version of Dahl's original argument. This is a perspective that shares the pluralistic view that competing interest groups shape political decision-making but does not, however, assume this to be the most fair and representative system. Moreover, neo-pluralism argues that some policies are, in fact, controlled by a very small number of interest groups. In this regard, it has become a synthesis between pluralist and elitist thought, though it is not always seen as such.

Author's Life

Robert A. Dahl was born in the city of Inwood, Iowa, in 1915. When he was 11, he and his family moved to Skagway, Alaska, where he lived until he was 21. Dahl earned a BA from the University of Washington in 1936 and a PhD from Yale University in 1940. He studied political science, and his dissertation, "Socialist Programs and Democratic

Politics: An Analysis," promoted market socialism,* an economic system in which the public owns the means of production. Though it was never published in its entirety, parts were later featured in Dahl's book *Democracy, Liberty, and Equality* (1986).

After completing his doctorate, Dahl served in the US Army during World War II* and was awarded the Bronze Star Medal; in 1946, he returned to Yale, where he would spend his academic career. In 1955, he was promoted to Eugene Meyer Professor of Political Science, and then to Sterling Professor of Political Science in 1964. He retired in 1986 in accordance with Yale University regulations, which allowed a maximum of 40 years of academic service. From then until his death in 2014, he was Sterling Professor Emeritus of Political Science. He remained active as an academic mentor until the final years of his life.

Dahl was also a member of the National Academy of Sciences, the American Philosophical Society, the American Academy of Arts and Sciences, as well as serving as president of the American Political Science Association. Two of his books, *Who Governs?* (1961) and *Democracy and Its Critics* (1989), received the prestigious Woodrow Wilson Foundation Award, an annual prize for the best book about American politics.

Today, Dahl is widely recognized as one of the great political scientists of the twentieth century. His work has transformed our understanding of how democracy works.

Author's Background

Robert A. Dahl spent his academic career studying and explaining the complexities of American democracy. In the preface of *Who Governs?* he claims that both elitist and pluralist scholars offer simplistic explanations of power, and that these explanations lack empirical evidence. He thus set out to fill this gap in the scholarly literature while also appealing to a general audience.

17

In 1955, Dahl reviewed the contemporary literature on American democracy at the Center for Advanced Study in the Behavioral Sciences in Palo Alto, California. Then, from 1957 to 1959, he conducted interviews and collected data in New Haven, Connecticut. Dahl chose New Haven for his case study because, in his view, its political system offered parallels to that of the nation. He hoped that his research at a local level would produce broader findings about how democracy worked nationally.

Dahl funded this project with grants from the Center for Advanced Study in the Behavioral Sciences, the Social Science Research Council, the Ford Foundation, and the American Philosophical Society and wrote most of the book while holding the research-only position of Ford Research Professor in the department of political science at Yale.

MODULE 2
ACADEMIC CONTEXT

KEY POINTS

- The major concern in 1961 at the time of publication of *Who Governs?* was the question of the distribution of power in American democracy.

- Robert A. Dahl published *Who Governs?* as a critical response to the political scientists Floyd Hunter* and C. Wright Mills,* whose belief that a small group of powerful individuals dictated politics and policy-making in America was typical of elite theory.*

- In *Who Governs?* Dahl both critiqued Hunter and Mills's methodology and called into question elite theory more broadly.

The Work in its Context

Robert A. Dahl's *Who Governs? Democracy and Power in an American City* was a response to a debate between elite and pluralist* theorists from 1951 to 1961 in which political scientists disagreed about the nature of American democracy. Elitists argued that a small group of influential individuals dominated politics and policy-making. In contrast, pluralists claimed that multiple interest groups struggled for power and influence, which in turn shaped policies and outcomes. After *Who Governs?* was published in 1961, pluralist theory became the dominant perspective on American democracy.

Dahl was influenced by the intellectual environment in which he lived and taught. He was serving as a professor at Yale University, where the pluralist theory of political science* held sway between 1955 and 1970. During that time, Yale's faculty members developed foundational

> ❝ Ironically, the very fact that democracy has such a lengthy history has actually contributed to confusion and disagreement, for 'democracy' has meant different things to different people at different times and places. ❞
>
> Robert A. Dahl, *On Democracy*

works of pluralism, and several, including the economist and political scientist Charles Lindblom* and Dahl himself, served as presidents of the American Political Science Association. The text emerged from the ideas of this community of scholars.

The timing and influence of the text should also be understood in relation to its broader backdrop. The long period of hostility between the United States and the Soviet Union* known as the Cold War* was at its height and as a consequence the question of whether American democracy was superior to Soviet communism,* a political system in which the state owns the means of production and social class is abolished, was considered important.

Overview of the Field

Who Governs? was a critical response to two key texts of elitist theory. The first was political scientist Floyd Hunter's *Community Power Structure* (1953), which argues that a small group of highly influential businessmen dominated politics and policy-making in Atlanta, Georgia. The second was C. Wright Mills's *The Power Elite* (1956), which claims that a combination of military, economic, and political elites—each with interconnecting interests—controls American decision-making. These scholars concluded that, in practice, America was undemocratic.

Dahl identifies flaws in the methodology of both of these texts, refutes their central claims, and offers a positive picture of American democracy. He does this by arguing, based on empirical* evidence, that politics in New Haven, Connecticut, were influenced by a suite of groups that competed to shape decisions rather than by a few powerful people. Furthermore, different groups influenced the making of different areas of policy. Dahl claims that these findings show American democracy to be pluralistic—although he also suggests that it should be compared to systems in other countries to better understand how it functions.

Since *Who Governs?* was published, Dahl has been the target of significant criticism. While he acknowledges obvious forms of power, he ignores more discrete forms, such as how politicians may decide on key issues behind closed doors (and therefore without the public's knowledge), and the ways in which powerful people subtly shape societal beliefs through the mass media.

Academic Influences
While at Yale, Dahl joined the behavioralist* revolution, a movement with significant influence in contemporary political science. Behavioralists investigated political behavior in American democracy, including voting, public opinion, legislative processes, and interest-group competition. The term "behavior" referred both to individual attitudes and to broader patterns of practice.

Dahl's methodological approach and argument in *Who Governs?* was influenced by Arthur F. Bentley* and David Truman,* two important political scientists and behavioralist scholars of the 1950s. Like Dahl, they were commonly referred to as "pluralists" because they argued that competition between interest groups characterized decision-making in the American political system. Dahl's case study was far more sophisticated than theirs, however, in that it reflected the American, two-party* federal system, and was grounded in two years of interviews, data collection, and analysis.

Dahl's positive view of American democracy, which differed from

Floyd Hunter and C. Wright Mills's pessimistic descriptions of a system controlled by a few wealthy people, was heavily influenced by Alexis de Tocqueville,* a French political theorist and commentator of the nineteenth century, whom he quotes repeatedly in his opening chapter. Tocqueville's *Democracy in America* (1835) is one of the most comprehensive books ever written on the subject. Like Tocqueville, Dahl believed that a pluralist system based on broad participation and competition among different interest groups was the healthiest and fairest system of government.

MODULE 3
THE PROBLEM

KEY POINTS

- When *Who Governs?* was published, political scientists had been trying to understand what power meant, who held it in America, and if the country was as democratic as it claimed to be.

- There were two competing perspectives on the distribution of power in American government: the elite* school and the pluralist* school.

- In *Who Governs?* Robert A. Dahl refuted the elitist claim and established pluralism as the dominant perspective on American democracy.

Core Question

The core question of Robert A. Dahl's *Who Governs? Democracy and Power in an American City* is "Who governs in a political system where nearly everyone can vote, but where political resources* that citizens can use to influence government policy are unequally distributed?"[1]

Dahl first points out that Americans widely believe that every citizen should have the same chance to influence government policy. He then explores who actually *can* influence political decisions. In doing so, he aims to clarify the nature of American democracy.

Dahl divides the core question into seven, more manageable, sub-questions:

- Do people who possess one type of resource (knowledge, wealth, or status, for example) also possess others?
- How are political decisions made?
- What kinds of people have the greatest influence on decisions?

> ❝ Over decades when political scientists focused on increasingly narrow and often technical questions, [Dahl's] the one person who brought everybody back to the big picture ... What is the form of democracy that will live up to democratic aspirations? ❞
>
> James S. Fishkin, "Robert A. Dahl Dies at 98; Yale Defined Politics and Power," *New York Times*

- Are all decisions made by the same people, and from what section of society do the most influential people come?
- Do leaders form one ruling group (oligarchic* leadership, in which only a few are in power), or do they divide, conflict, and bargain (pluralistic leadership)?
- What is the relative importance of the right to vote?
- Are the patterns of influence lasting or changing, and how does the belief of ordinary citizens in equality and democracy affect the operation of the political system?[2]

Dahl explores these questions in the context of New Haven, Connecticut. While he acknowledges that no city exactly represents all others, he claims that New Haven is, in many respects, a typical American city because it embodies most of the equalities and inequalities he explores.[3] As he puts it, while the "political system of New Haven falls short of the usual conception of an ideal democracy ... [it] is an example of a democratic system, warts and all."[4]

The Participants

Dahl's argument was shaped by the intellectual and political context of his time. The work was published in 1961, in the midst of the Cold War* tension between the United States and the communist Soviet Union* during which the US championed around the world its own form of government, liberal democracy* (a political system that emphasizes human and civil rights, and regular and free elections between competing political parties). In this context, a scholarly debate emerged over the nature of the American system, in which the elite and pluralist theories competed to explain how power and influence operated.

Dahl had first refuted elite theory in *A Preface to Democratic Theory* (1956), in which he argued that modern democracies should be thought of as polyarchies,* or open, competitive, and pluralist systems whose leaders needed to account for the preferences of different interest groups.[5] In *Who Governs?* he goes further, providing empirical* evidence that no single elite group held decision-making positions in New Haven. Instead, he claims, a variety of different groups compete for power. While *Who Governs?* echoes many of the conclusions from *A Preface to Democratic Theory*, it attracted far more attention because it was grounded in a case study and in verifiable data. Ultimately, *Who Governs?* established pluralism as the foremost perspective on American democracy.

The Contemporary Debate

Who Governs? was part of Dahl's ongoing debate with his scholarly adversary, the political scientist C. Wright Mills.* In *The Power Elite* (1956), an important text in elite theory, Mills argued that military, corporate, and political elites had interwoven interests and dominated political decision-making in the United States.[6] These actors tended to study and have strong contact bases in the country's most prestigious universities, including Harvard, Yale, and Princeton. Furthermore, Mills claimed that ordinary citizens were largely powerless to shape politics, and were easily manipulated by powerful actors.

In *Who Governs?*, Dahl refutes Mill's elite theory by arguing that a variety of groups compete to influence the decision-making process. The book also rebuts the work of another elite theorist, Floyd

25

Hunter.* In 1953, Hunter published *Community Power Structure*, which argued that a power elite dominated the city of Atlanta, Georgia.[7] Drawing on interviews, Hunter suggested that power was concentrated among a few business owners, top executives, and corporate lawyers who lived in the same neighborhood, belonged to the same clubs, and sat on each other's boards of directors.

NOTES

1   Robert A. Dahl, *Who Governs? Democracy and Power in an American City*, 2nd ed. (New Haven: Yale University Press, 2005), 1.

2   Dahl, *Who Governs?*, 7–8.

3   Dahl, *Who Governs?*, xiii, 4.

4   Dahl, *Who Governs?*, 311.

5   Robert A. Dahl, *A Preface to Democratic Theory* (Chicago: University of Chicago Press, 1956).

6   C. Wright Mills, *The Power Elite*, 2nd ed. (New York: Oxford University Press, 2000).

7   Floyd Hunter, *Community Power Structure: A Study of Decision Makers* (Chapel Hill: University of Carolina Press, 1953).

MODULE 4
THE AUTHOR'S CONTRIBUTION

KEY POINTS

- Robert A. Dahl argues that the American political system is pluralist*—one in which different groups compete for power and shape policy-making.

- *Who Governs?* builds on previous pluralist scholarship, including Dahl's own 1956 study, and positions pluralism as the dominant perspective from which to view American democracy.

- Dahl achieves this by empirically* testing pluralist theory in New Haven, Connecticut, and then applying his findings to American democracy as a whole.

Author's Aims

In the preface to the original 1961 edition of *Who Governs? Democracy and Power in an American City*, Robert A. Dahl specifies that he has three audiences in mind: the academic community, the citizens of the greater New Haven area, and readers who wish to "gain a greater understanding of their own communities, American politics, or even democracy itself."[1] Dahl acknowledges that these audiences may differ in terms of interests and background.

The text successfully reached and influenced these audiences. It had an immense effect on American political science, encouraging many to see democracy as pluralist. In fact, some of Dahl's students would become important actors in American politics. Among these were George W. Bush,* US president from 2001 to 2009; Dick Cheney,* Bush's vice president; and Joseph Lieberman,* who served as Connecticut senator from 1989 to 2013.

> ❝ Instead of a single center of sovereign power, there must be multiple centers of power, none of which is or can be wholly sovereign. ❞
>
> Robert A. Dahl, *Pluralist Democracy in the United States*

However, one need not have political science training to understand *Who Governs?* With clear and accessible ideas and language, the text also shaped the ideas of the public, particularly the view that American liberal democracy* was superior to Soviet* communism* during the Cold War.*

Approach

Dahl's aim is to determine who governs in a political system where, although everyone is able to vote, there also exist profound, unequal distributions of power resources such as economic wealth, knowledge, and social standing.[2] *Who Governs?* answers this aim systematically.

In Book I, Dahl argues that over the past 200 years, New Haven has changed from an oligarchy* (a system of government in which a small group of people holds power) to a polyarchy* (a system in which different groups possess different resources and influence). In Book II, Dahl proceeds to examine how influence is distributed, concluding that while only a few people can *directly* influence policy, voters in elections *indirectly* influence the decisions politicians make through public opinion.

In Book III, Dahl explores patterns of specialized influence in New Haven, finding that different people influence different sectors of public activity, and that people who persuade these sectors come from a variety of social strata. This is a system of dispersed inequalities: citizens use varying kinds of resources, which are unequally distributed, to influence officials. An influence resource* (a resource that can be mobilized to influence government policy-making) that is effective in one area is often not effective in another. Almost no one entirely lacks influence resources.[3]

In Book IV, Dahl discusses how different political resources* (specifically social standing, access to credit and cash, access to public office, popularity and jobs, and control over information) are distributed. And in Book V, he examines how these resources are used.

Dahl finds that citizens use their political resources to varying extents, explaining this as the gap between their *actual* and *potential* influence. Most citizens use their resources for purposes other than gaining influence over government decisions. Dahl argues that, in pluralistic political systems, politics "is a sideshow in the great circus of life."[4] Most citizens are not very politically active, so the number of highly influential citizens is a small segment of the population.

In Book VI, he rates New Haven's pluralistic democratic system as very stable, asserting also that leaders must make their appeals consistent with the democratic beliefs of the ordinary citizens who vote for them.[5]

Contribution in Context

Who Governs? was an important contribution to behavioralism* and, by showing that power in American democracy was fragmented, to pluralist theory. Pluralism originates from Dahl's *A Preface to Democratic Theory* (1956), in which he launched several hypotheses on how the American political system worked. He dismissed two common theories of democracy: Madisonian theory,* which states that the majority must be prevented from depriving minorities of their rights through institutional mechanisms, and populist theory,* according to which democracy is based on majority rule. According to Dahl, neither theory captured how modern democracies operate.

A theory of democracy, Dahl argued, had to be based on reality and not ideals. He therefore suggested a number of conditions that could be measured. If a political system fulfilled these conditions, it could be called a polyarchal, or pluralist, democracy. However, Dahl did not have any empirical evidence for how real democracies in the world operated, which is why he felt compelled to conduct empirical research.[6] *Who Governs?* can be understood as Dahl testing the theory developed in his *Preface to Democratic Theory* to see if the American political system was truly democratic.

NOTES

1   Robert A. Dahl, *Who Governs? Democracy and Power in an American City* (New Haven: Yale University Press, 1961), xv.

2   Robert A. Dahl, *Who Governs? Democracy and Power in an American City,* 2nd ed. *(New Haven: Yale University Press, 2005), 1.*

3   Dahl, *Who Governs?, 228.*

4   Dahl, *Who Governs?*, 305.

5   Dahl, *Who Governs?*, 324–5.

6   Nelson W. Polsby, "Robert A. Dahl," in *Political Science in America: Oral Histories of a Discipline*, ed. Michael A. Baer et al. (Lexington: University Press of Kentucky, 1991).

SECTION 2
IDEAS

MODULE 5
MAIN IDEAS

KEY POINTS

- The three main ideas of *Who Governs?* are: America has changed over the past 200 years from an oligarchic* to a pluralist* system; power consists of being able to influence others to do what you want; and people shape politics indirectly, even if they do not participate directly.

- Robert A. Dahl's main argument is that competing interest groups shape politics and policy-making in America.

- In targeting an academic, local (specifically New Haven, Connecticut), and general audience, the author presents these ideas in a clear and accessible way

Key Themes

There are three main themes in Robert A. Dahl's *Who Governs?* The first is that, over the past 200 years, America has changed from an oligarchic to a pluralist system. In an oligarchy, a few select people accumulate sources of influence. This means that these few people are able to influence many different social and economic fields of decision-making. In a pluralist system, however, sources of influence are dispersed. No single source of influence is decisive in all or even a majority of decisions. Different groups therefore influence different areas of decision-making.

The second main theme is that political power is the ability to influence (that is, to make someone else do what you want). Influence resources,* such as wealth, high social standing, access to cash or credit, access to public office, popularity, occupation, and control over information, can therefore be seen as political resources.* These

> 66 There are many nuances and variations in the
> warp of power as Dahl traces it, but it never in any
> instance resembles the static hierarchy described in the
> conventional wisdom that preceded *Who Governs?* 99
>
> Douglas Rae, foreword to the second edition of *Who Governs? Democracy and Power in an American City*

resources are distributed unequally, but almost no one lacks them entirely. Additionally, different political resources are effective in different policy fields.

The third theme is that the majority of people are apolitical (that is, they take no interest in politics). Only an active minority, made up of professional politicians and members of the political stratum, directly affect policies. The apolitical mass, however, still indirectly affects politics, since leaders must shape their platforms to the preferences of voters. As a result, even though many people do not directly take part in political decision-making, their opinions still matter.

Exploring the Ideas

These three themes emerge logically and coherently in Dahl's case study of New Haven. He begins by providing historical evidence that the city has changed from an oligarchy to pluralism. He then examines three areas of decision-making in contemporary New Haven: nominations for office, public education, and urban renewal. His study reveals that in each of these, different groups influence policy.

Finally, Dahl shows that citizens vary in the way they use influence resources. Many are not engaged in politics and, therefore, use their resources for other purposes. As a consequence, the number of politically influential citizens is small. Elections, however, cause leaders to shape their platforms in accordance with public opinion, and therefore many citizens do *indirectly* influence decisions. Even apolitical people have power, since power, Dahl argues, is the ability to influence the behavior of others. Together, these ideas show how the American liberal democratic* system, with its emphasis on regular and free elections between competing political parties, is pluralist.

Language and Expression

Who Governs? is written in language that is clear and accessible to academic, local, and general audiences. Although it employs specialized terms, as Dahl acknowledges in his preface, it does not alienate the layperson.

One particularly important specialist term is polyarchy,* which refers to open, competitive, and pluralist political systems in which competing interest groups use power and influence to shape politics and policy-making. Dahl believes this is essential to democracy because it prevents a small group of elites* from dominating society. Dahl's definition of power is also significant: "A has power over B to the extent that he can get B to do something that B would not otherwise do."[1] This has served as an important foundation for subsequent debate in political science.

Throughout the book, Dahl tries to identify with the citizens of New Haven by referring to local entities such as the United Illuminating Company, Southern New England Telephone Company, and Malley's, the department store. Furthermore, he analyzes issues that affect everyone, such as income, public opinion, and voting, and shows the way citizens influence politics both directly and indirectly.

NOTES

1   Robert A. Dahl, "The Concept of Power," *Behavioral Science* 2, no. 3 (1957): 203.

MODULE 6
SECONDARY IDEAS

KEY POINTS

- The most important secondary theme in *Who Governs?* is Robert A. Dahl's definition of power.
- Dahl's definition of power has served as a foundation for subsequent scholarship and debate in political science.
- Dahl's broader argument is that American democracy is characterized by shared power among different, competing actors.

Other Ideas

Robert A. Dahl's definition of power is the most important secondary theme in *Who Governs? Democracy and Power in an American City*. For Dahl, power is the ability to get others to do what you want. Professors require students to write essays or take exams, for example, in order to receive grades. Although students might not want to do these things, they are likely to comply because if they do not, they will fail. The same is true of paying taxes. Although some people would prefer not to pay taxes, they pay them anyway because of the legal consequences of not doing so. This is the concept of overt power that Dahl stresses.

An example from *Who Governs?* is Dahl's study of urban renewal in New Haven, in which he demonstrates how the mayor was able to carry out his plans for the city by influencing a wide range of community actors. In this case, he was much more powerful than corporate elites.

This definition of power has proved useful to academics. It has provided an important foundation against which competing understandings have developed.

> ❝ Power and influence have been the center of the field of the study of politics from the beginning. And what's more, they are the central elements in all of our lives ... and they're enormously complex. ❞
>
> Robert A. Dahl and Margaret Levi, "A Conversation with Robert A. Dahl"

Exploring the Ideas

Dahl's definition of power followed previous scholarship by the political theorists Harold Lasswell* and Herbert Simon,* who had defined power as the ability to cause changes.[1] In 1957, Dahl phrased this as "A has power over B to the extent that he can get B to do something that B would otherwise not do"[2]—the definition that lies at the core of *Who Governs?* Dahl puts it into practice by looking at the influence that different interest groups had over decision-making processes in New Haven.

Dahl's focus on political processes followed the work of the behavioralist* political scientists Arthur F. Bentley* and David Truman.*[3] He adopted their basic assumption of what constituted power and influence but modified it in certain ways (he believed Bentley and Truman overemphasized the importance of politicians, for example). In *Who Governs?,* Dahl highlights how the choices made by individual citizens—who they vote for, for example—also have important consequences for policy.

Overlooked

Who Governs? is one of the most significant works of modern political science and has been subject to thorough scholarly scrutiny since its publication in 1961.[4] In his notably coherent text, Dahl argues (as we have seen) that the American liberal democratic* system is a pluralist* system in which many different groups influence different areas of policy-making. He argues that people have different sources of influence, each of which is effective in a different policy-making area. Although most citizens use their resources for other purposes than influencing government, the decisions of the minority directly involved in politics reflect the values and goals of the apolitical majority. In consequence, these ideas all contribute to describing the pluralist system and none can be said to have been overlooked.

Who Governs? describes the distribution of power in the American liberal democratic system. As this system is still in place today, it cannot really be said to invite reconsideration.

NOTES

1   Harold D. Lasswell and Abraham Kaplan, *Power and Society: A Framework for Political Inquiry* (New Haven: Yale University Press, 1950); Herbert A. Simon, "Notes on the Observation and Measurement of Political Power," *Journal of Politics* 15, no.4 (1953): 500–16.

2   Robert A. Dahl, "The Concept of Power," *Behavioral Science*, no. 3 (1957): 203.

3   Arthur F. Bentley, *The Process of Government: A Study of Social Pressures* (Chicago: University of Chicago Press, 1908); David B. Truman, *The Governmental Process* (New York: Knopf, 1951).

4   For example, *A New Handbook of Political Science,* Robert E. Goodin and Hans-Dieter Klingemann, eds, (Oxford: Oxford University Press, 1996) includes *Who Governs?* among around 20 post-World War II publications that are part of the language of political science.

MODULE 7
ACHIEVEMENT

KEY POINTS

- By publishing *Who Governs?*, Robert A. Dahl positioned pluralism* as the dominant perspective in the study of American democracy.

- He was able to achieve this because he supported his claim with empirical* data.

- *Who Governs?* was subject to considerable criticism.

Assessing the Argument

In *Who Governs? Democracy and Power in an American City*, Robert A. Dahl finds that the local upper-class are not the same people who make up the local business community. He then reconstructs how decisions are made by looking at who influences whom in three different areas: nominations for political office, urban redevelopment, and public education. He concludes that many groups influence policies, and that elected and appointed government officials, especially the mayor, are key decision-makers. Meanwhile, neither the wealthiest citizens nor the business community are any more involved in decisions than other interest groups. Although the business community is sometimes able to block policies with which it disagrees, it does not initiate or shape policy in any significant way.

Dahl stresses four key elements of his study:

- Power is the ability to use one's influence to change the behavior of others.

- Political scientists need to study what power is, and who has it, through the construction of the sorts of empirical case studies called for by the behavioralist* approach.

> 66 What did Hunter and Mills say that was upsetting to mainstream social scientists and journalists? They simply concluded that an elite few—business elites for Hunter, or a combination of corporate, government, and military elites for Mills—dominate local and national governments in the United States in a very direct way. 99
>
> William Domhoff, "C. Wright Mills, Floyd Hunter, and 50 Years of Power Structure Research" Keynote address to the Michigan Sociological Association, 2006

- Power is not necessarily distributed the same way in different areas of political policy.
- Power must be understood in terms of the particular goals of given actors.

Dahl's fieldwork in New Haven shows that American democracy is not dominated by a small group of actors but is a pluralist system in which several groups compete for influence and shape politics.

Achievement in Context

Arguably the most influential political scientist of the twentieth century, Dahl's theories of power and democracy are still commonly taught in introductory courses in political science. Together with critiques of power, they serve as important foundations for debate. His concept of polyarchy,* or pluralism, is also a key concept for understanding how democracy works, especially in the United States.

In addition to his achievements in political science, Dahl will be remembered as: a behavioralist, for a research practice founded on evidence that can be verified by observation; a pluralist, for his emphasis on fragmented power; and as someone who enhanced the reputation of political science at Yale University, where he researched, taught, and mentored for more than 60 years. In addressing the author's legacy, the renowned political scientist Ian Shapiro★ recently commented: "He really created modern Yale political science, as well as the modern discipline of political science. ... If there were a Nobel Prize for political science he would have gotten the first one."[1] This is a clear testament to the depth and reach of Dahl's influence.

Limitations

After its publication, *Who Governs?* was continuously dismissed by elite* theorists, who believed that power was concentrated in the hands of a few people. The most vocal of these critics was William Domhoff,* who contested Dahl's view in his 1967 book *Who Rules America?*[2] and then went on to re-do Dahl's research in New Haven, which resulted in an updated 1978 book, *Who Really Rules? New Haven and Community Power Reexamined*.[3] In this provocative text, dedicated to the scholar and elitist theorist Floyd Hunter,* Domhoff argues that the elected officials of New Haven play only a minor role in policy formation because the New Haven power structure is concentrated in the banks, the Chamber of Commerce, and Yale University. Domhoff's findings suggest that the upper class controls the government through wealth, media, education, and their policy-making agenda. Domhoff continues to contest Dahl's conclusions in updated editions of *Who Rules America*,[4] arguing that a cohesive upper class in the United States exercises a disproportionate share of power through political and economic decisions.

Dahl's main target in *Who Governs?*, the sociologist C. Wright Mills, died before he could respond.

NOTES

1   Cited in Adrian Rodrigues and Matthew Lloyd-Thomas, "Dahl's Legacy Remembered," *Yale Daily News*, February 7, 2014, accessed May 21, 2015, http://yaledailynews.com/blog/2014/02/07/dahls-legacy-remembered/.

2   G. William Domhoff, *Who Rules America?* (Englewood Cliffs: Prentice-Hall, 1967).

3   G. William Domhoff, *Who Really Rules? New Haven and Community Power Reexamined* (New Brunswick: Transaction Books, 1978).

4   G. William Domhoff, *Who Rules America Now? A View for the '80s*, 2nd ed. (Englewood Cliffs: Prentice-Hall, 1983); *Who Rules America? Power and Politics in the Year 2000*, 3rd ed. (Mountain View: Mayfield, 1998); *Who Rules America? Power, Politics, and Social Change*, 5th ed. (New York: McGraw-Hill, 2005); *Who Rules America? Challenges to Corporate and Class Dominance*, 6th ed. (New York: McGraw-Hill, 2009); *Who Rules America? The Triumph of the Corporate Rich*, 7th ed. (New York: McGraw-Hill, 2013).

MODULE 8
PLACE IN THE AUTHOR'S WORK

KEY POINTS

- Robert A. Dahl's body of work is a consistent, progressive analysis of power and influence in American democracy.

- *Who Governs?*, an empirical* assessment of power, was one of several seminal works in the author's extraordinary number of publications.

- Dahl will be remembered as one of the most influential political scientists of the twentieth century and a champion of democracy in theory and practice.

Positioning

The publication of *Who Governs? Democracy and Power in an American City* in 1961 established Robert A. Dahl as a leading proponent of the approaches to political science known as behavioralism* and pluralism.* The text fits with Dahl's other important works from roughly the same period, most notably *A Preface to Democratic Theory* (1956)[1] and *Pluralist Democracy in the United States: Conflict and Consent* (1967).[2] In these books, Dahl developed his description of the American political system.

In *A Preface*, he generated a number of hypotheses on how American democracy worked. Among these was his theory of polyarchy,* which referred to existing modern democracies rather than idealistic theories of democracy. In *Who Governs?*, Dahl used empirical research about the way power is distributed in society to show how the American political system actually worked. In *Pluralist Democracy*, Dahl offered a descriptive account of American democracy and theorized about the way conflicts between citizens that threatened

> 66 Robert Dahl is one of the most renowned American political scientists of the twentieth century, with a long and distinguished career at Yale University. From his association in the 1950s and 1960s with the behavioral movement in political science to his recent work, Dahl's corpus forms a relentless and strikingly consistent analysis of the nature and workings of contemporary—predominantly American—democracy. 99
>
> Henrik Enroth, *Encyclopedia of Political Theory*

the political order could be prevented.

Dahl wrote prolifically throughout his long career and certain of his publications offer revisions of some of his early conclusions. As his scholarly reputation was defined by his work in the 1960s, however, *Who Governs?* remains crucial to understanding his career as a whole. He published his last book in 2006 at the age of 89.

Integration

Who Governs? is part of Dahl's long-standing research on polyarchy, a concept introduced by Dahl and the political scientist Charles E. Lindblom* in their jointly written *Politics, Economics, and Welfare* (1953) and further developed in Dahl's *A Preface to Democratic Theory* (1956). *Who Governs?* provides empirical evidence to show how a polyarchic system works. It anticipates Dahl's later works such as *Polyarchy: Participation and Opposition* (1971), which examines the conditions under which a polyarchic system can be introduced.

In *Democracy and Its Critics* (1989), Dahl brings together 50 years of research. He distinguishes between democracy as a utopian ideal—that is, a perfect political, legal, and social system—and democracy as it exists in practice, which is inevitably flawed.[3] Later in his academic career, Dahl wrote *How Democratic is the American Constitution?* (2002), in which he praises the writers of that deeply influential document setting out the laws and principles of the US government, while at the same time arguing that the modern-day United States has not adopted the necessary amendments to account for the way conditions have changed. He also compares and contrasts the American political system with other democracies around the world.

Significance

Dahl's work explores democratic institutions and practices. Each successive text builds on and extends previous works. Throughout his academic career, he has attempted to make sense of democracy both in America and abroad. Although he has written many different works over many decades, he sees his body of work as a unified whole. In a 1991 interview, he said: "In fact, I'm a little worried sometimes about that: that it's all one big, long book. I'm always astonished when people see these great discontinuities. I think it's quite the other way around."[4]

It is essential to note, however, that over time Dahl has modified and refined his conclusions from the 1960s, which largely defended the existing political system. His later works, which responded both to critics and political developments, were more pessimistic in their view of the American system.

Dahl's career can be seen as a systematic attempt to understand and explain American democracy. This approach began with the presentation of his pluralist argument. In responding to his critics he refined that argument, and analyzed the degree to which the US Constitution is democratic, considering ways in which America has failed in comparison to other democratic nations and prescribing ways in which it might be improved.

NOTES

1   Robert A. Dahl, *A Preface to Democratic Theory* (Chicago: University of Chicago Press, 1956).

2   Robert A. Dahl, *Pluralist Democracy in the United States: Conflict and Consent* (Chicago: Rand McNally, 1967).

3   Robert A. Dahl, *On Democracy* (New Haven: Yale University Press, 1998).

4   Nelson W. Polsby, "Interview with Robert A. Dahl," in *Political Science in America: Oral Histories of a Discipline*, ed. Michael A. Baer et al. (Lexington: University Press of Kentucky, 1991), 175.

SECTION 3
IMPACT

MODULE 9
THE FIRST RESPONSES

KEY POINTS

- The psychologist and sociologist William Domhoff* became the most prominent critic of Robert A. Dahl by repeating his study in New Haven and drawing different conclusions.

- Although Dahl refined his argument over time in response to criticism and ongoing developments, he always defended his pluralist* view of American democracy.

- *Who Governs?* was acknowledged as important because of the strong empirical* base of Dahl's study and the seminal definitions of power and pluralism it contained.

Criticism

Although Robert A. Dahl's *Who Governs? Democracy and Power in an American City* was received favorably, this reception was not unanimous. Critics claimed that Dahl ignored the role of citizen participation in a democratic system. In his "A Critique of the Elitist Theory of Democracy" (1966), for example, the political scientist Jack L. Walker* argued that the pluralist approach failed to account for important changes in American society caused by political movements that had gained momentum in the 1960s.[1] These, he charged, emerged from social frustrations that were left out of the pluralist framework.

Another criticism was that there was no great difference between Dahl's findings and those of "elitist"* studies[2] since, in Dahl's study, only a few people influence political decision-making. Dahl does not, however, refer to these people as "elite," arguing that the apolitical majority still influences politics—though he does not provide empirical evidence to support this. It may not be surprising to learn

❝ It may be that the most serious criticism I can make of Dahl is that he never should have done this interview-based study in the first place, for it was doomed from the start to fall victim to the ambitions and plans of the politicians, planners, lawyers, and businessmen that he was interviewing. ❞

William Domhoff, "Robert A. Dahl Yale Professor and Political Scientist Who Wrote *On Democracy* Dies at 98," *Washington Post*

that political scientist Floyd Hunter, in his earlier study of Atlanta, Georgia, *Community Power Structure* (1953), noticed many of the same things as Dahl—but interpreted them as evidence for elitism.

There were other negative responses. For example, critics questioned whether New Haven, Connecticut, was representative of the United States in general. While they acknowledged that New Haven was typical of old industrial centers in economic decay, they also noted that it differed from cities experiencing economic booms, such as Houston, Texas.

Responses

In his book *After the Revolution? Authority in a Good Society* (1970),[3] Dahl addressed issues of democracy and governance, evaluating alternative forms of democracy. Although he maintained that there was no ideal form, he concluded that participatory forms of democracy were best.

In the late 1970s, Dahl engaged in a critical dialogue with the influential psychologist and sociologist William Domhoff, who had reconducted Dahl's research in New Haven in his book *Who Really Rules? New Haven and Community Power Reexamined* (1978).[4] Domhoff had concluded that the banks, the Chamber of Commerce, and Yale University were highly influential in governing the city. Furthermore, he maintained that external forces such as the business elite initiated policy-making, while elected officials played only a minor role, mainly by popularizing and promoting policies. Dahl responded in a review article,[5] charging that Domhoff failed to provide enough proof for his claims.

Dahl did not significantly revise *Who Governs?* as a result of criticism. In the preface to the second edition, published in 2005, he reflects that his approach, which had been to interview people who had participated in different decisions, had been "fruitful."[6] He does write, however, that "changes in New Haven and in my own views about how to search for answers to the question of 'who governs?' would result, today, I imagine, in a different book."[7]

Conflict and Consensus

Who Governs? was a pluralist response to elite theory and helped pluralism become the dominant perspective within political science. Elitist scholars have continued to challenge *Who Governs?*, though these critiques have not fundamentally swayed general perceptions of the book.[8] These critics remain focused on challenging Dahl's assertion that a variety of different groups influence political decisions, charging instead that the policy-making process in America is driven by a small group of powerful individuals.

Today, *Who Governs?* is generally considered to be less relevant to the field of political science than it once was. Dahl's main aim of disproving the theory that a power elite controls policy-making is no longer an important area of research. That said, *Who Governs?* continues to influence contemporary political science in its relevance for neo-pluralist* theory. In addition to Dahl's basic assumption of the existence of different interest groups, neo-pluralist theory considers to be important in such matters as: agenda building (who gets to determine the political agenda); the logic of collective action (the idea that small groups of producers form lobbies to pursue their interests in particular areas of policy-making); and social movements.

NOTES

1   Jack L. Walker, "A Critique of the Elitist Theory of Democracy," *American Political Science Review* 60, no. 2 (1966) 2: 285–95.

2   Floyd Hunter, "Review of *Who Governs? Democracy and Power in an American City*, by Robert A. Dahl," *Administrative Science Quarterly* 6, no. 4 (1962): 517–19.

3   Robert A. Dahl, *After the Revolution? Authority in a Good Society* (New Haven: Yale University Press, 1970).

4   G. William Domhoff, *Who Really Rules? New Haven and Community Power Reexamined* (New Brunswick: Transaction Books, 1978).

5   Robert A. Dahl, "Review of Who Really Rules? New Haven and Community Power Reexamined, by G. William Domhoff," Social Science Quarterly 60 (1979): 144–51.

6   Robert A. Dahl, *Who Governs? Democracy and Power in an American City*, 2nd ed. (New Haven: Yale University Press, 2005), xi.

7   Dahl, *Who Governs?*, xii.

8   See, for example, the works of G. William Domhoff: *Who Really Rules? New Haven and Community Power Reexamined* (New Brunswick: Transaction Books, 1978); G. William Domhoff, *Who Rules America Now? A View for the '80s*, 2nd ed. (Englewood Cliffs: Prentice-Hall, 1983); *Who Rules America? Power and Politics in the Year 2000*, 3rd ed. (Mountain View: Mayfield, 1998); *Who Rules America? Power, Politics, and Social Change*, 5th ed. (New York: McGraw-Hill, 2005); *Who Rules America? Challenges to Corporate and Class Dominance,* 6th ed. (New York: McGraw-Hill, 2009); *Who Rules America? The Triumph of the Corporate Rich*, 7th ed. (New York: McGraw-Hill, 2013); and those of Thomas R. Dye: *Who's Running America? Institutional Leadership in the United States* (Englewood Cliffs: Prentice-Hall, 1976); *Who's Running America? The Carter Years* (Englewood Cliffs: Prentice-Hall, 1979); *Who's Running America? The Reagan Years* (Englewood Cliffs: Prentice-Hall, 1983); *Who's Running America? The Conservative Years* (Englewood Cliffs: Prentice-Hall, 1986); *Who's Running America? The Bush Era* (Englewood Cliffs: Prentice Hall, 1990); *Who's Running America? The Clinton Years* (Englewood Cliffs: Prentice Hall, 1995); *Who's Running America? The Bush Restoration* (Englewood Cliffs: Prentice Hall, 2002); and Thomas R. Dye, Louis Schubert and Harmon Zeigler, *The Irony of Democracy: An Uncommon Introduction to American Politics* (London: Wadsworth Publishing Company, 2013).

MODULE 10
THE EVOLVING DEBATE

KEY POINTS

- Robert A. Dahl's concepts of power and pluralist*
  democracy continue to be foundational in political science.

- They will also likely continue to be points of reference for
  future scholarship and debate.

- Neo-pluralism* is a modernized version of Dahl's original thesis.

Uses and Problems

Robert A. Dahl's *Who Governs? Democracy and Power in an American City* has been particularly important to the evolution of political science. First, after its publication, Dahl's theory of pluralism prevailed over that of elitism* in mainstream political science. Second, the book has been hailed as among the most important works on power.

Today neo-pluralism*, a theory that has evolved from Dahl's pluralism, is part of the mainstream within political science and public policy research. Although there are currently varying interpretations on who controls power, some neo-pluralists have shown that there are more varied interest groups now than there were 50 years ago.[1] One possible explanation for this is that interest groups have become more important since they began to play a greater role in funding politicians' campaigns.[2]

Schools of Thought

Who Governs? is a foundational pluralist text. The ideas it contains were widely taken up and employed in American political science during the 1960s. Influential pluralists included Seymour Martin Lipset,* who studied comparative democracy and was known for linking democracy with economic growth, Nelson Polsby,* who studied the

> **❝** Originating from Robert Dahl's pluralism model in
> *Who Governs?* (1961), neopluralism evolved in the study
> of American politics through discarding or modifying
> some of Dahl's ideas, while adding new concerns. **❞**
>
> Andrew McFarland, "Neopluralism"

US presidency and Congress,* and Raymond Wolfinger,* an expert
on voter behavior.

Towards the end of the 1960s, the influence of pluralism waned as
the theory came under heavy criticism. One important critic, the
economics professor Mancur Olson,* argued in *The Logic of Collective
Action: Public Goods and the Theory of Groups* (1965) that there were
multiple independent elites* in the United States, each controlling
different policy areas.[3] Olson maintained that, since lobbies make
public policies available to all individuals, people are not likely to
contribute to the lobby but instead act as "free riders." Collective
action is therefore unlikely to occur unless group members receive
selective incentives.

In response to Olson's critique, the theory of neo-pluralism
emerged between 1975 and 1985. Like pluralist theory, neo-pluralist
theory posits that multiple interest groups compete to influence
different areas of policy. It does not, however, equate the existence of
interest groups with fair representation. Neo-pluralists acknowledge
that while some policy areas are sites of struggle between different
groups, others are ruled by a single, elite coalition or just a few groups.
Some leading voices include the political scientist Andrew
McFarland,* an expert on interest groups, public policy, and political
participation, and Christopher Bosso* and Lawrence Rothenberg,*
both scholars of environmental policy.

In Current Scholarship

Pluralist scholars share several basic premises; they argue that political power is distributed among competing groups; that policy-makers are not proactive, rather they respond to public demands; that different political leaders generally build coalitions with different interest groups; and that this process brings about gradual political change. *Who Governs?* brought these assumptions together in a single framework.

While *Who Governs?* was a study of local politics, other pluralists applied Dahl's ideas to a range of subjects within American politics. For example, Nelson Polsby, a former graduate student of Dahl's at Yale University, examined political institutions from a behavioralist* and pluralist perspective and stressed the evolving nature of fragmented power in American democracy.[4] Gabriel Almond,* a professor and colleague of Dahl's at Yale University, investigated democracy and political cultures and pioneered comparative methods of studying democracy, particularly between the United States and Europe.[5] And Fred I. Greenstein,* also a former graduate student of Dahl's, compared democratic presidents and political parties.[6]

These studies help provide a comprehensive image of political behavior and how power is distributed and exercised.

NOTES

1   Jack L. Walker, *Mobilizing Interest Groups in America: Patrons, Professions, and Social Movements* (Ann Arbor: University of Michigan Press, 1991).

2   L. Sandy Maisel and Jeffrey M. Berry, eds, *The Oxford Handbook of American Political Parties and Interest Groups* (Oxford: Oxford University Press, 2010).

3   Mancur Olson, *The Logic of Collective Action: Public Goods and the Theory of Groups* (Cambridge: Harvard University Press, 2009).

4   Nelson W. Polsby, "Legislatures," in *Handbook of Political Science*, ed. Fred I. Greenstein and Nelson W. Polsby (Reading, MA: Addison-Wesley, 1975), 257–319.

5   Gabriel A. Almond and Sidney Verba, *The Civic Culture: Political Attitudes and Democracy in Five Nations* (Newbury Park, CA: Sage Publications, 1989).

6   Fred I. Greenstein, *The American Party System and the American People* (Englewood Cliffs: Prentice-Hall, 1963).

MODULE 11
IMPACT AND INFLUENCE TODAY

KEY POINTS

- *Who Governs?* remains influential in our understanding of how power and democracy operate in the United States and elsewhere.

- The text continues to pose a formidable challenge to proponents of elite* theory.

- Neo-pluralism,* a modernized version of Dahl's original thesis, is the dominant perspective on power and democracy today.

Position

Robert A. Dahl's *Who Governs? Democracy and Power in an American City* has influenced both academics and politicians. In academia, it formed the foundation for scholarship and debate on democracy, especially with regard to the American system. Its definition of overt power (the power to influence others to do what one wants) has since been significantly expanded to account for more discrete forms of control. Furthermore, Dahl's pluralist* understanding of democracy has been modernized and refined into neo-pluralism, the dominant perspective in political science today. These concepts are commonly taught as fundamentals to those beginning their studies in the field of political science.

Several of Dahl's former students at Yale University have become prominent politicians. Examples include former presidents Bill Clinton* and George W. Bush,* former vice president Dick Cheney,* former senator Joseph Lieberman,* and former New York senator and secretary of state Hillary Clinton.* These figures were influenced both

> ❝ [Robert A. Dahl] really created modern Yale political
> science, as well as the modern discipline of political
> science ... If there were a Nobel Prize for political
> science he would have gotten the first one. ❞
>
> Ian Shapiro, *Yale Daily News*

by Dahl and other Yale pluralists, such as the great scholar of
comparative democracy Gabriel Almond.*

Further, Dahl helped construct a positive and progressive image of
American democracy during the Cold War,* during which tensions
between the US and the communist Soviet Union* were high. He
was successful in part because he delivered his message in clear,
accessible language to both an academic and general audience.

Interaction

Though *Who Governs?* made pluralism the dominant perspective
within political science, elite theory remains relevant in modern
political science and sociology. For example, Robert Putnam,* a
Harvard University professor of public policy, argues in *The
Comparative Study of Political Elites* (1976) that elected government
officials and technical advisers influence public policy-making in a
way that undermines the democratic process.[1] Thomas Dye* and
Harmon Zeigler,* two influential contemporary elite theorists, argue
in *The Irony of Democracy* (2011) that elites govern all societies because
they control resources that are unavailable to most people.[2]

It is important, however, to note that these theorists contest, but do
not necessarily invalidate, the points Dahl made in *Who Governs?* since
elitists and pluralists use similar empirical evidence to argue different
viewpoints. There is no significant difference between Dahl's findings
and the findings of contemporary elitist studies—which indicates that

ideological differences account for the differing interpretations. Dahl does not see the leaders he finds as "elites." While he acknowledges that only a few people directly influence policy-making, he also argues that different groups of citizens have different means for exerting influence. Although these resources are unequally distributed, no influence resource* such as money or public support dominates all others, and virtually no citizen entirely lacks influence resources.[3]

The Continuing Debate

Today, the majority of mainstream political science and public policy research is based on neo-pluralist assumptions. Neo-pluralism shares Dahl's basic assumption that the political domain contains a range of interest groups.

Neo-pluralism has been influenced by sociology and economics. From sociology, it has taken the idea that social movements lead to the formation of interest groups. It also employs network theory,* which examines the structure of communication between different actors. Neo-pluralism has derived insights from the economist Mancur Olson,* who argued in *The Logic of Collective Action* (1965) that, since lobbies make public policies available to all, people most likely will not contribute to lobbies but instead act as free riders. Under these circumstances, collective action is unlikely to occur.[4] This contemporary debate stretches beyond the confines of political science

Today, elitist scholars continue to challenge the arguments made in *Who Governs?* Thomas Dye, for example, an influential contemporary elitist theorist, has examined American leadership, including the administrations of former presidents Richard Nixon,* Gerald Ford,* and George W. Bush. Mapping the leaders heading American institutions, he found that the process of policy-making was indeed led by elites.

NOTES

1   Robert D. Putnam, *The Comparative Study of Political Elites* (Englewood Cliffs: Prentice-Hall, 1976).

2   Thomas R. Dye, Louis Schubert and Harmon Zeigler, *The Irony of Democracy: An Uncommon Introduction to American Politics* (London: Wadsworth Publishing Company, 2011).

3   Robert A. Dahl, *Who Governs? Democracy and Power in an American City*, 2nd ed. (New Haven: Yale University Press, 2005), 228.

4   Mancur Olson, *The Logic of Collective Action: Public Goods and the Theory of Groups* (Cambridge, MA: Harvard University Press, 2009).

MODULE 12
WHERE NEXT?

KEY POINTS

- It is likely that *Who Governs?* will remain foundational in the study of power and democracy.
- Neo-pluralism* will likely continue to be an important perspective for understanding modern democracies.
- Neo-pluralism represents a foundation upon which different aspects of political behavior and political institutions can be studied.

Potential

We can expect Robert A. Dahl's *Who Governs?*, being the foundation for contemporary studies of the nature of governmental power, to remain a notably influential work of modern political science. That said, Dahl's pluralist theory* is considered outdated, and it is unlikely that the core ideas of *Who Governs?* will be further developed—except perhaps within a neo-pluralist framework.

Today, there is a much greater emphasis on comparing American democracy with that of other developed nations and assessing the degree to which democracies live up to their ideals. This will offer deeper insight into how to improve democracy. It is fair to say that Dahl's writing and ideas inspired this sort of research.

Future Directions

Dahl's definition of power provided an important foundation against which competing social science definitions have developed. For example, in 1962 the political scientist Peter Bachrach* and the economist Morton Baratz* proposed that power has "two faces." They

> ❝ Neither the prevailing consensus, the creed, nor even the political system itself are immutable products of democratic, ideas, beliefs, and institutions inherited from the past. For better or worse, they are always open, in some measure, to alteration through those complex processes of symbiosis and change that constitute the relations of leaders and citizens in a pluralist democracy. ❞
>
> Robert A. Dahl, *Who Governs? Democracy and Power in an American City*

referred to Dahl's definition of power—that is, that power means using resources to change the behavior of others—as the first, or overt, face of power. They then argued that there is a second, covert face of power: the ability to control the decision-making agenda—that is, to control which issues are considered important and to prevent others from being considered at all.[1] In 1974, the sociologist Steven Lukes* added a third dimension. In addition to overt and covert power, Lukes's model contained a *latent* dimension: the ability to make people believe they have certain interests, even if those "interests" actually harm them.[2] Further research will likely be carried out in this area.

Another concept that has attracted scholars since the 1990s is "issue framing,"* a term that refers to the way that interest groups frame or label issues that affect policy outcomes. A public-health group, for example, can frame a tax on tobacco positively or negatively, thereby shaping whether or not this tax is adopted. Robert Benford* and David Snow* have famously argued that understanding who frames which issue is crucial to understanding policy-making within a particular policy area.[3] This idea, which originates from Dahl's pluralist perspective, is likely to be the subject of further research and discussion.

While it is unlikely that issues other than these from *Who Governs?* will be considered important in the future, the text will likely continue to be taught to students of political science because it is foundational; all students of the field should at least be aware of it.

Summary

Robert A. Dahl's *Who Governs?* was a key text during the behavioralist* revolution in the field of political science of the 1950s and 1960s. It established pluralism—a theory that states that competing interest groups shape politics and policy-making—as the dominant perspective on American democracy. This challenged Floyd Hunter* and C. Wright Mills's* theory of elitism,* which had been the prevailing school of thought. Since publication, the text has been criticized for its methodology and argument. These critiques have led to a modernized, refined perspective known as neo-pluralism, which today represents the most common understanding of power and democracy. The neo-pluralist school is derived from Dahl's basic premise that politics is shaped by competing interest groups; however, it is more critical of American democracy, and emphasizes that certain policy areas are, in fact, dominated by a select number of elite actors or interest groups.

Robert A. Dahl was one of the great political scientists of the twentieth century, and his work will likely continue to remain relevant in academic debate. In more than 60 years' service at Yale University, he made immense contributions to the study of democracy and has left behind a legacy that few will equal.

NOTES

1   Peter *Bachrach* and Morton S. *Baratz*, "Two Faces of Power,"" *American Political Science Review* 56, no. 4 (*1962*): 947–52.

2   Steven Lukes, *Power: A Radical View* (London: Macmillan, 1974).

3   Robert D. Benford, and David A. Snow, "Framing Processes and Social Movements: An Overview and Assessment," *Annual Review of Sociology* 26 (2000): 611–39.

GLOSSARY

GLOSSARY OF TERMS

Behavioralism: a scientific approach to political science that came to the fore between 1951 and 1961. Its proponents investigated contemporary political behavior in America, including voting, public opinion, legislative behavior, and interest groups.

Cold War: the military rivalry and political tension that defined relations between, on the one hand, the United States, NATO (the North Atlantic Treaty Organization) and their allied countries, and on the other, the USSR (the Union of Soviet Socialist Republics) and the Warsaw Pact, between 1947 and 1991.

Communism: a political ideology founded on state ownership of the means of production, the collectivization of labor, and the abolition of social class.

Elite theory/elitism: the theory that only a small, non-representative portion of society dominates politics and policy-making.

Empiricism: the belief that knowledge should come from evidence verifiable by observation and not from theory or logic.

Influence resource: any resource that can be mobilized to influence government policy-making—for example, money or public support.

Issue framing: refers to the way that interest groups frame or label issues that affect policy outcomes.

Liberal democracy: a political system that emphasizes human and civil rights, regular and free elections between competing political parties, and adherence to the rule of law.

Madisonian theory: a system of government in which power is separated into three branches of government: legislative, executive, and judicial.

Market socialism: an economic system that involves the public ownership of the means of production within the framework of the market economy.

Meritocracy: a system in which people progress on the basis of ability and talent rather than on the basis of class privilege or wealth.

Neo-pluralism: a theory sharing Dahl's assumption that politics is determined by different, competing interest groups but does not, however, assume that this leads to the most fair and representative system. In fact, it emphasizes that some policy areas are controlled by either a single coalition of actors or a few interest groups.

Network theory: the study of asymmetrical structures and hierarchies. It is an interdisciplinary approach that is sometimes used to explain social and political organizations.

Oligarchy: a political system in which power is concentrated in the hands of a few people.

Political resources: according to Dahl, these are resources that people can use to influence others. Examples are: wealth, income, education, status, knowledge, popularity, and organization.

Pluralism: a political system in which power is distributed among multiple groups.

Polyarchy: a term coined by Dahl that refers to a pluralist system (a system in which power is vested in multiple interest groups).

Populist theory: the theory that a democratic system is based on majority rule.

Soviet Union: the Union of Soviet Socialist Republics (USSR) was a union of 15 communist republics in Eastern Europe and Central and North Asia that existed between 1917 and 1991.

Two-party system: a system in which a country's politics are dominated by two major parties, such as the Democrats and Republicans in the United States.

US Constitution: a document adopted in 1787 and ratified in 1789 that acts as the supreme law of the United States of America.

US Congress: the legislative (that is, law-making) body of the United States federal government.

World War II: a global conflict lasting from 1939 to 1945 that was fought between the Axis Powers (Germany, Italy, and Japan) and the victorious Allied Powers (the United Kingdom and its colonies, the Soviet Union, and the United States).

PEOPLE MENTIONED IN THE TEXT

Gabriel Almond (1911–2002) was professor of political science at Yale University and a pioneer of comparative research on democracies.

Peter Bachrach (1918–2007) was professor emeritus of political science at Temple University. With Morton Baratz, he co-authored "Two Faces of Power" (1962), which built on the work of Robert A. Dahl.

Morton S. Baratz (1924–98) was an instructor in economics at Yale University. With Peter Bachrach, he co-authored "Two Faces of Power" (1962), which built on the work of Robert A. Dahl.

Robert Benford is professor of sociology at the University of South Florida. He is a scholar of social movements, war and peace, social psychology, and the sociology of sport.

Arthur F. Bentley (1870–1957) was an American political scientist who helped develop the behavioralist approach to political science.

Christopher Bosso is professor of public policy and urban affairs at Northeastern University.

George W. Bush (b. 1946) was the 43rd president of the United States from 2001 to 2009.

Richard (Dick) Cheney (b. 1941) is an American politician and businessman. He was vice president of the United States from 2001 to 2009.

Hillary Rodham Clinton (b. 1947) is an American politician. The wife of Bill Clinton, she is a former New York Senator and secretary of state. She was a student of Robert A. Dahl's at Yale University.

William Jefferson (Bill) Clinton (b. 1946) was the 42nd president of the United States from 1993 to 2001. He is the husband of Hillary Clinton.

William Domhoff (b. 1936) is professor of psychology and sociology at the University of California at Santa Cruz. He repeated Robert A. Dahl's study in New Haven, Connecticut, and drew different conclusions.

Thomas Dye (b. 1935) is emeritus professor of political science and an expert on democracy at Florida State University.

Henrik Enroth is senior lecturer (associate professor) of political science at Linnaeus University

James Fishkin (b. 1948) is professor of political science at Stanford University and an expert on democracy.

Gerald Ford (1913–2006) was the 38th president of the United States from 1974 to 1977.

Fred I. Greenstein (b. 1930) is professor emeritus of politics and an expert on presidential politics at Yale University.

Floyd Hunter (1912–92) was a social worker, community activist, professor, and author. His most important work was *Community Power Structure* (1953), which argued that elitist theory described how power was exercised in Atlanta, Georgia.

Harold Lasswell (1902–78) was professor of law at Yale University and an expert on political behavior.

Joseph Lieberman (b. 1942) is an American politician and former senator for Connecticut. He is a former student of Robert A. Dahl at Yale University.

Charles E. Lindblom (b. 1917) is an American political scientist and economist who formerly served as director of Yale University's Institution of Social and Policy Studies.

Seymour Martin Lipset (1922–2006) was a senior fellow at the Hoover Institution at Stanford University and Hazel professor of public policy at George Mason University. He was an expert on democracy.

Steven Lukes (b. 1941) is professor of politics and sociology at New York University. He is the author of *Power: A Radical View* (2005).

Andrew McFarland is professor of political science at the University of California at Berkeley. He is an expert on public policy, interest groups, social movements, and political participation.

C. Wright Mills (1916–62) was an American sociologist who had an important influence on the American New Left, a leftist movement in the US and UK in the 1960s and 1970s that sought to provide a revisionist Marxist alternative to what it perceived as the authoritarianism of the communist bloc.

Richard Nixon (1913–94) was the 37th president of the United States from 1969 to 1974.

Mancur Olson (1932–98) was professor of economics at the University of Maryland, College Park. He was an expert on interest group formation, among other subjects.

Nelson Polsby (1934–2007) was professor of political science at the University of California at Berkeley. He was an expert on the United States presidency and Congress.

Robert Putnam (b. 1941) is the Malkin Professor of Public Policy at Harvard University John F. Kennedy School of Government. He is an expert on democracy.

Lawrence Rothenberg is the Corrigan-Minehan Professor of Political Science at the University of Rochester. He is an expert on legislative politics, interest groups, and environmental and public policy.

Ian Shapiro (b. 1956) is the Sterling Professor of Political Science at Yale University. He is an expert on democracy and justice.

Herbert Simon (1916–2001) was a political scientist, economist, psychologist, computer scientist and Richard King Mellon Professor at Carnegie Mellon University.

David Snow is distinguished professor of sociology at the University of California, Irvine. He is a scholar of social movements, social psychology, and qualitative field methods.

Alexis de Tocqueville (1805–59) was a French political thinker. In 1835, he wrote *Democracy in America*, a notable early text on the subject.

David Truman (1913–2003) was an American political scientist who contributed to developing the behavioralist approach to political science.

Jack L. Walker Jr. (1935–90) was professor and chair of political science at the University of Michigan. He was an expert on interest group and policy formation.

Raymond Wolfinger (1931–2015) was professor emeritus of political science at the University of California at Berkeley. He is best known for co-authoring the book *Who Votes?* (1980).

Harmon Ziegler (1936–2006) was the Philip M. Phibbs Distinguished Professor of American Politics at the University of Puget Sound and affiliate professor at the University of Washington.

WORKS CITED

WORKS CITED

Almond, Gabriel A. and Sidney Verba. *The Civic Culture: Political Attitudes and Democracy in Five Nations*. Newbury Park: Sage Publications, 1989.

Bachrach, Peter and Morton S. *Baratz*. "Two Faces of Power." *American Political Science Review* 56, no. 4 (*1962*): 947–52.

Benford, Robert D. and David A. Snow. "Framing Processes and Social Movements: An Overview and Assessment." *Annual Review of Sociology* 26 (2000): 611–39.

Bentley, Arthur F. *The Process of Government*: *A Study of Social Pressures.* Chicago: University of Chicago Press, 1908.

Dahl, Robert A. *After the Revolution? Authority in a Good Society*. New Haven: Yale University Press, 1970.

——— "The Concept of Power." *Behavioral Science* 2, no. 3 (1957): 202–3.

——— *Democracy and Its Critics*. New Haven: Yale University Press. 1989.

——— *Democracy, Liberty, and Equality* (1986). Oslo: Norwegian University Press, 1986.

_____ *How Democratic is the American Constitution?* New Haven: Yale University Press, 2002.

_____ *On Democracy*. New Haven: Yale University Press, 1998.

_____ *Pluralist Democracy in the United States: Conflict and Consent*. Chicago: Rand McNally, 1967.

_____ *Polyarchy: Participation and Opposition*. New Haven: Yale University Press, 1971.

_____ *A Preface to Democratic Theory*. Chicago: University of Chicago Press, 1956.

———"Review of *Who Really Rules? New Haven and Community Power Reexamined* by G. William Domhoff." *Social Science Quarterly* 60, no. 1 (1979): 144–51.

_____ "Socialist Programs and Democratic Politics: An Analysis." PhD diss., Yale University, 1940.

——— *Who Governs? Democracy and Power in an American City*. 2nd ed. New Haven: Yale University Press, 2005.

Dahl, Robert A. and Charles Edward Lindblom. *Politics, Economics, and Welfare*. Chicago: University of Chicago Press, 1953.

Dahl, Robert A. and Margaret Levi. "A Conversation with Robert A. Dahl." *Annual Review of Political Science* 12 (2009): 1–9.

Domhoff, G. William. *Who Really Rules? New Haven And Community Power Reexamined*. New Brunswick: Transaction Books, 1978.

_____ *Who Rules America?* Englewood Cliffs: Prentice-Hall, 1967.

_____ *Who Rules America? Challenges to Corporate and Class Dominance*. 6th ed. New York: McGraw-Hill, 2009.

_____ *Who Rules America Now? A View for the '80s*. 2nd ed. Englewood Cliffs: Prentice-Hall, 1983.

_____ *Who Rules America? Power and Politics in the Year 2000*. 3rd ed. Mountain View: Mayfield, 1998.

_____ *Who Rules America? Power, Politics, and Social Change*. 5th ed. New York: McGraw-Hill, 2005.

_____ *Who Rules America? The Triumph of the Corporate Rich*, 7th ed. New York: McGraw-Hill, 2013.

_____ "C. Wright Mills, Floyd Hunter, and 50 Years of Power Structure Research," Keynote address to the Michigan Sociological Association, 2006. Accessed September 7, 2015. http://www2.ucsc.edu/whorulesamerica/theory/mills_address.html.

Dye, Thomas R. *Who's Running America? The Bush Era*. Englewood Cliffs: Prentice Hall, 1990.

_____ *Who's Running America? The Bush Restoration*. Englewood Cliffs: Prentice Hall, 2002.

_____ *Who's Running America? The Carter Years*. Englewood Cliffs: Prentice-Hall, 1979.

_____ *Who's Running America? The Clinton Years*. Englewood Cliffs: Prentice Hall, 1995.

_____ *Who's Running America? The Conservative Years*. Englewood Cliffs: Prentice-Hall, 1986.

——— *Who's Running America? Institutional Leadership in the United States*. Englewood Cliffs: Prentice-Hall, 1976.

_____ *Who's Running America? The Reagan Years*. Englewood Cliffs: Prentice-Hall, 1983.

Dye, Thomas R., Louis Schubert and Harmon Zeigler. *The Irony of Democracy: An Uncommon Introduction to American Politics*. London: Wadsworth, 2013.

Enroth, Henrik. "Robert Dahl." In *Encyclopedia of Political Theory*, edited by Mark Bevir, 349–50. London: Sage, 2010.

Goodin, Robert E. and Hans-Dieter Klingemann, eds. *A New Handbook of Political Science*. Oxford: Oxford University Press, 1996.

Greenstein, Fred I. *The American Party System and the American People*. Englewood Cliffs: Prentice-Hall, 1963.

Hunter, Floyd. *Community Power Structure: A Study of Decision Makers*. Chapel Hill: University of North Carolina Press, 1953.

_____ "Review of *Who Governs? Democracy and Power in an American City*, by Robert A. Dahl." *Administrative Science Quarterly* 6, no. 4 (1962): 517–19.

Italie, Hillel. "Robert A. Dahl Yale Professor and Political Scientist Who Wrote on Democracy Dies at 98." *Washington Post*, February 8, 2014. Accessed May 24, 2015. http://www.washingtonpost.com/national/robert-a-dahl-yale-professor-and-political-scientist-who-wrote-on-democracy-dies-at-98/2014/02/08/505b4140-9012–11e3–b46a-5a3d0d2130da_story.html.

Lasswell, Harold D. and Abraham Kaplan. *Power and Society: A Framework for Political Inquiry.* New Haven: Yale University Press, 1950.

Lukes, Steven. *Power: A Radical View*. London: Macmillan, 1974.

Maisel, L. Sandy and Jeffrey M. Berry, eds. *The Oxford Handbook of American Political Parties and Interest Groups*. Oxford: Oxford University Press, 2010.

Martin, Douglas. "Robert A. Dahl Dies at 98; Yale Scholar Defined Politics and Power." *New York Times*, February 7, 2014. Accessed May 24, 2015. http://www.nytimes.com/2014/02/08/us/politics/robert-a-dahl-dies-at-98-defined-politics-and-power.html.

McFarland, Andrew S. "Neopluralism," *Annual Review of Political Science* 10 (2007): 45–66.

Mills, C. Wright. *The Power Elite*. New York: Oxford University Press, 1956.

Olson, Mancur. *The Logic of Collective Action: Public Goods and the Theory of Groups*. Cambridge, MA: Harvard University Press, 1965.

Polsby, Nelson W. "Robert A. Dahl." In *Political Science in America: Oral Histories of a Discipline*, edited by Michael A. Baer, Malcolm Edwin Jewell and Lee Sigelman. Lexington: University Press of Kentucky, 1991.

_____ "Legislatures." In *Handbook of Political Science*, edited by Fred I. Greenstein and Nelson W. Polsby. Reading: Addison-Wesley, 1975, 257–319.

Putnam, Robert D. *The Comparative Study of Political Elites.* Englewood Cliffs: Prentice-Hall, 1976.

Rodrigues Adrian and Matthew Lloyd-Thomas. "Dahl's Legacy Remembered." *Yale Daily News*, February 7, 2014. Accessed May 21, 2015. http://yaledailynews.com/blog/2014/02/07/dahls-legacy-remembered/.

Simon, Herbert A. "Notes on the Observation and Measurement of Political Power." *Journal of Politics* 15, no. 4 (1953): 500–16.

Tocqueville, Alexis de. *Democracy in America*. Translated by Gerald E. Bevan. London: Penguin, 2003.

Truman, David B. *The Governmental Process*. New York: Knopf, 1951.

Walker, Jack L. "A Critique of the Elitist Theory of Democracy." *American Political Science Review* 60, no. 2 (1966) 2: 285–95.

——— *Mobilizing Interest Groups in America: Patrons, Professions, and Social Movements*. Ann Arbor: University of Michigan Press, 1991.

THE MACAT LIBRARY
BY DISCIPLINE

The Macat Library By Discipline

AFRICANA STUDIES

Chinua Achebe's *An Image of Africa: Racism in Conrad's Heart of Darkness*
W. E. B. Du Bois's *The Souls of Black Folk*
Zora Neale Huston's *Characteristics of Negro Expression*
Martin Luther King Jr's *Why We Can't Wait*
Toni Morrison's *Playing in the Dark: Whiteness in the American Literary Imagination*

ANTHROPOLOGY

Arjun Appadurai's *Modernity at Large: Cultural Dimensions of Globalisation*
Philippe Ariès's *Centuries of Childhood*
Franz Boas's *Race, Language and Culture*
Kim Chan & Renée Mauborgne's *Blue Ocean Strategy*
Jared Diamond's *Guns, Germs & Steel: the Fate of Human Societies*
Jared Diamond's *Collapse: How Societies Choose to Fail or Survive*
E. E. Evans-Pritchard's *Witchcraft, Oracles and Magic Among the Azande*
James Ferguson's *The Anti-Politics Machine*
Clifford Geertz's *The Interpretation of Cultures*
David Graeber's *Debt: the First 5000 Years*
Karen Ho's *Liquidated: An Ethnography of Wall Street*
Geert Hofstede's *Culture's Consequences: Comparing Values, Behaviors, Institutes and Organizations across Nations*
Claude Lévi-Strauss's *Structural Anthropology*
Jay Macleod's *Ain't No Makin' It: Aspirations and Attainment in a Low-Income Neighborhood*
Saba Mahmood's *The Politics of Piety: The Islamic Revival and the Feminist Subject*
Marcel Mauss's *The Gift*

BUSINESS

Jean Lave & Etienne Wenger's *Situated Learning*
Theodore Levitt's *Marketing Myopia*
Burton G. Malkiel's *A Random Walk Down Wall Street*
Douglas McGregor's *The Human Side of Enterprise*
Michael Porter's *Competitive Strategy: Creating and Sustaining Superior Performance*
John Kotter's *Leading Change*
C. K. Prahalad & Gary Hamel's *The Core Competence of the Corporation*

CRIMINOLOGY

Michelle Alexander's *The New Jim Crow: Mass Incarceration in the Age of Colorblindness*
Michael R. Gottfredson & Travis Hirschi's *A General Theory of Crime*
Richard Herrnstein & Charles A. Murray's *The Bell Curve: Intelligence and Class Structure in American Life*
Elizabeth Loftus's *Eyewitness Testimony*
Jay Macleod's *Ain't No Makin' It: Aspirations and Attainment in a Low-Income Neighborhood*
Philip Zimbardo's *The Lucifer Effect*

ECONOMICS

Janet Abu-Lughod's *Before European Hegemony*
Ha-Joon Chang's *Kicking Away the Ladder*
David Brion Davis's *The Problem of Slavery in the Age of Revolution*
Milton Friedman's *The Role of Monetary Policy*
Milton Friedman's *Capitalism and Freedom*
David Graeber's *Debt: the First 5000 Years*
Friedrich Hayek's *The Road to Serfdom*
Karen Ho's *Liquidated: An Ethnography of Wall Street*

John Maynard Keynes's *The General Theory of Employment, Interest and Money*
Charles P. Kindleberger's *Manias, Panics and Crashes*
Robert Lucas's *Why Doesn't Capital Flow from Rich to Poor Countries?*
Burton G. Malkiel's *A Random Walk Down Wall Street*
Thomas Robert Malthus's *An Essay on the Principle of Population*
Karl Marx's *Capital*
Thomas Piketty's *Capital in the Twenty-First Century*
Amartya Sen's *Development as Freedom*
Adam Smith's *The Wealth of Nations*
Nassim Nicholas Taleb's *The Black Swan: The Impact of the Highly Improbable*
Amos Tversky's & Daniel Kahneman's *Judgment under Uncertainty: Heuristics and Biases*
Mahbub Ul Haq's *Reflections on Human Development*
Max Weber's *The Protestant Ethic and the Spirit of Capitalism*

FEMINISM AND GENDER STUDIES

Judith Butler's *Gender Trouble*
Simone De Beauvoir's *The Second Sex*
Michel Foucault's *History of Sexuality*
Betty Friedan's *The Feminine Mystique*
Saba Mahmood's *The Politics of Piety: The Islamic Revival and the Feminist Subject*
Joan Wallach Scott's *Gender and the Politics of History*
Mary Wollstonecraft's *A Vindication of the Rights of Women*
Virginia Woolf's *A Room of One's Own*

GEOGRAPHY

The Brundtland Report's *Our Common Future*
Rachel Carson's *Silent Spring*
Charles Darwin's *On the Origin of Species*
James Ferguson's *The Anti-Politics Machine*
Jane Jacobs's *The Death and Life of Great American Cities*
James Lovelock's *Gaia: A New Look at Life on Earth*
Amartya Sen's *Development as Freedom*
Mathis Wackernagel & William Rees's *Our Ecological Footprint*

HISTORY

Janet Abu-Lughod's *Before European Hegemony*
Benedict Anderson's *Imagined Communities*
Bernard Bailyn's *The Ideological Origins of the American Revolution*
Hanna Batatu's *The Old Social Classes And The Revolutionary Movements Of Iraq*
Christopher Browning's *Ordinary Men: Reserve Police Batallion 101 and the Final Solution in Poland*
Edmund Burke's *Reflections on the Revolution in France*
William Cronon's *Nature's Metropolis: Chicago And The Great West*
Alfred W. Crosby's *The Columbian Exchange*
Hamid Dabashi's *Iran: A People Interrupted*
David Brion Davis's *The Problem of Slavery in the Age of Revolution*
Nathalie Zemon Davis's *The Return of Martin Guerre*
Jared Diamond's *Guns, Germs & Steel: the Fate of Human Societies*
Frank Dikotter's *Mao's Great Famine*
John W Dower's *War Without Mercy: Race And Power In The Pacific War*
W. E. B. Du Bois's *The Souls of Black Folk*
Richard J. Evans's *In Defence of History*
Lucien Febvre's *The Problem of Unbelief in the 16th Century*
Sheila Fitzpatrick's *Everyday Stalinism*

Eric Foner's *Reconstruction: America's Unfinished Revolution, 1863-1877*
Michel Foucault's *Discipline and Punish*
Michel Foucault's *History of Sexuality*
Francis Fukuyama's *The End of History and the Last Man*
John Lewis Gaddis's *We Now Know: Rethinking Cold War History*
Ernest Gellner's *Nations and Nationalism*
Eugene Genovese's *Roll, Jordan, Roll: The World the Slaves Made*
Carlo Ginzburg's *The Night Battles*
Daniel Goldhagen's *Hitler's Willing Executioners*
Jack Goldstone's *Revolution and Rebellion in the Early Modern World*
Antonio Gramsci's *The Prison Notebooks*
Alexander Hamilton, John Jay & James Madison's *The Federalist Papers*
Christopher Hill's *The World Turned Upside Down*
Carole Hillenbrand's *The Crusades: Islamic Perspectives*
Thomas Hobbes's *Leviathan*
Eric Hobsbawm's *The Age Of Revolution*
John A. Hobson's *Imperialism: A Study*
Albert Hourani's *History of the Arab Peoples*
Samuel P. Huntington's *The Clash of Civilizations and the Remaking of World Order*
C. L. R. James's *The Black Jacobins*
Tony Judt's *Postwar: A History of Europe Since 1945*
Ernst Kantorowicz's *The King's Two Bodies: A Study in Medieval Political Theology*
Paul Kennedy's *The Rise and Fall of the Great Powers*
Ian Kershaw's *The "Hitler Myth": Image and Reality in the Third Reich*
John Maynard Keynes's *The General Theory of Employment, Interest and Money*
Charles P. Kindleberger's *Manias, Panics and Crashes*
Martin Luther King Jr's *Why We Can't Wait*
Henry Kissinger's *World Order: Reflections on the Character of Nations and the Course of History*
Thomas Kuhn's *The Structure of Scientific Revolutions*
Georges Lefebvre's *The Coming of the French Revolution*
John Locke's *Two Treatises of Government*
Niccolò Machiavelli's *The Prince*
Thomas Robert Malthus's *An Essay on the Principle of Population*
Mahmood Mamdani's *Citizen and Subject: Contemporary Africa And The Legacy Of Late Colonialism*
Karl Marx's *Capital*
Stanley Milgram's *Obedience to Authority*
John Stuart Mill's *On Liberty*
Thomas Paine's *Common Sense*
Thomas Paine's *Rights of Man*
Geoffrey Parker's *Global Crisis: War, Climate Change and Catastrophe in the Seventeenth Century*
Jonathan Riley-Smith's *The First Crusade and the Idea of Crusading*
Jean-Jacques Rousseau's *The Social Contract*
Joan Wallach Scott's *Gender and the Politics of History*
Theda Skocpol's *States and Social Revolutions*
Adam Smith's *The Wealth of Nations*
Timothy Snyder's *Bloodlands: Europe Between Hitler and Stalin*
Sun Tzu's *The Art of War*
Keith Thomas's *Religion and the Decline of Magic*
Thucydides's *The History of the Peloponnesian War*
Frederick Jackson Turner's *The Significance of the Frontier in American History*
Odd Arne Westad's *The Global Cold War: Third World Interventions And The Making Of Our Times*

The Macat Library By Discipline

LITERATURE

Chinua Achebe's *An Image of Africa: Racism in Conrad's Heart of Darkness*
Roland Barthes's *Mythologies*
Homi K. Bhabha's *The Location of Culture*
Judith Butler's *Gender Trouble*
Simone De Beauvoir's *The Second Sex*
Ferdinand De Saussure's *Course in General Linguistics*
T. S. Eliot's *The Sacred Wood: Essays on Poetry and Criticism*
Zora Neale Huston's *Characteristics of Negro Expression*
Toni Morrison's *Playing in the Dark: Whiteness in the American Literary Imagination*
Edward Said's *Orientalism*
Gayatri Chakravorty Spivak's *Can the Subaltern Speak?*
Mary Wollstonecraft's *A Vindication of the Rights of Women*
Virginia Woolf's *A Room of One's Own*

PHILOSOPHY

Elizabeth Anscombe's *Modern Moral Philosophy*
Hannah Arendt's *The Human Condition*
Aristotle's *Metaphysics*
Aristotle's *Nicomachean Ethics*
Edmund Gettier's *Is Justified True Belief Knowledge?*
Georg Wilhelm Friedrich Hegel's *Phenomenology of Spirit*
David Hume's *Dialogues Concerning Natural Religion*
David Hume's *The Enquiry for Human Understanding*
Immanuel Kant's *Religion within the Boundaries of Mere Reason*
Immanuel Kant's *Critique of Pure Reason*
Søren Kierkegaard's *The Sickness Unto Death*
Søren Kierkegaard's *Fear and Trembling*
C. S. Lewis's *The Abolition of Man*
Alasdair MacIntyre's *After Virtue*
Marcus Aurelius's *Meditations*
Friedrich Nietzsche's *On the Genealogy of Morality*
Friedrich Nietzsche's *Beyond Good and Evil*
Plato's *Republic*
Plato's *Symposium*
Jean-Jacques Rousseau's *The Social Contract*
Gilbert Ryle's *The Concept of Mind*
Baruch Spinoza's *Ethics*
Sun Tzu's *The Art of War*
Ludwig Wittgenstein's *Philosophical Investigations*

POLITICS

Benedict Anderson's *Imagined Communities*
Aristotle's *Politics*
Bernard Bailyn's *The Ideological Origins of the American Revolution*
Edmund Burke's *Reflections on the Revolution in France*
John C. Calhoun's *A Disquisition on Government*
Ha-Joon Chang's *Kicking Away the Ladder*
Hamid Dabashi's *Iran: A People Interrupted*
Hamid Dabashi's *Theology of Discontent: The Ideological Foundation of the Islamic Revolution in Iran*
Robert Dahl's *Democracy and its Critics*
Robert Dahl's *Who Governs?*
David Brion Davis's *The Problem of Slavery in the Age of Revolution*

Alexis De Tocqueville's *Democracy in America*
James Ferguson's *The Anti-Politics Machine*
Frank Dikotter's *Mao's Great Famine*
Sheila Fitzpatrick's *Everyday Stalinism*
Eric Foner's *Reconstruction: America's Unfinished Revolution, 1863-1877*
Milton Friedman's *Capitalism and Freedom*
Francis Fukuyama's *The End of History and the Last Man*
John Lewis Gaddis's *We Now Know: Rethinking Cold War History*
Ernest Gellner's *Nations and Nationalism*
David Graeber's *Debt: the First 5000 Years*
Antonio Gramsci's *The Prison Notebooks*
Alexander Hamilton, John Jay & James Madison's *The Federalist Papers*
Friedrich Hayek's *The Road to Serfdom*
Christopher Hill's *The World Turned Upside Down*
Thomas Hobbes's *Leviathan*
John A. Hobson's *Imperialism: A Study*
Samuel P. Huntington's *The Clash of Civilizations and the Remaking of World Order*
Tony Judt's *Postwar: A History of Europe Since 1945*
David C. Kang's *China Rising: Peace, Power and Order in East Asia*
Paul Kennedy's *The Rise and Fall of Great Powers*
Robert Keohane's *After Hegemony*
Martin Luther King Jr.'s *Why We Can't Wait*
Henry Kissinger's *World Order: Reflections on the Character of Nations and the Course of History*
John Locke's *Two Treatises of Government*
Niccolò Machiavelli's *The Prince*
Thomas Robert Malthus's *An Essay on the Principle of Population*
Mahmood Mamdani's *Citizen and Subject: Contemporary Africa And The Legacy Of Late Colonialism*
Karl Marx's *Capital*
John Stuart Mill's *On Liberty*
John Stuart Mill's *Utilitarianism*
Hans Morgenthau's *Politics Among Nations*
Thomas Paine's *Common Sense*
Thomas Paine's *Rights of Man*
Thomas Piketty's *Capital in the Twenty-First Century*
Robert D. Putman's *Bowling Alone*
John Rawls's *Theory of Justice*
Jean-Jacques Rousseau's *The Social Contract*
Theda Skocpol's *States and Social Revolutions*
Adam Smith's *The Wealth of Nations*
Sun Tzu's *The Art of War*
Henry David Thoreau's *Civil Disobedience*
Thucydides's *The History of the Peloponnesian War*
Kenneth Waltz's *Theory of International Politics*
Max Weber's *Politics as a Vocation*
Odd Arne Westad's *The Global Cold War: Third World Interventions And The Making Of Our Times*

POSTCOLONIAL STUDIES

Roland Barthes's *Mythologies*
Frantz Fanon's *Black Skin, White Masks*
Homi K. Bhabha's *The Location of Culture*
Gustavo Gutiérrez's *A Theology of Liberation*
Edward Said's *Orientalism*
Gayatri Chakravorty Spivak's *Can the Subaltern Speak?*

PSYCHOLOGY

Gordon Allport's *The Nature of Prejudice*
Alan Baddeley & Graham Hitch's *Aggression: A Social Learning Analysis*
Albert Bandura's *Aggression: A Social Learning Analysis*
Leon Festinger's *A Theory of Cognitive Dissonance*
Sigmund Freud's *The Interpretation of Dreams*
Betty Friedan's *The Feminine Mystique*
Michael R. Gottfredson & Travis Hirschi's *A General Theory of Crime*
Eric Hoffer's *The True Believer: Thoughts on the Nature of Mass Movements*
William James's *Principles of Psychology*
Elizabeth Loftus's *Eyewitness Testimony*
A. H. Maslow's *A Theory of Human Motivation*
Stanley Milgram's *Obedience to Authority*
Steven Pinker's *The Better Angels of Our Nature*
Oliver Sacks's *The Man Who Mistook His Wife For a Hat*
Richard Thaler & Cass Sunstein's *Nudge: Improving Decisions About Health, Wealth and Happiness*
Amos Tversky's *Judgment under Uncertainty: Heuristics and Biases*
Philip Zimbardo's *The Lucifer Effect*

SCIENCE

Rachel Carson's *Silent Spring*
William Cronon's *Nature's Metropolis: Chicago And The Great West*
Alfred W. Crosby's *The Columbian Exchange*
Charles Darwin's *On the Origin of Species*
Richard Dawkin's *The Selfish Gene*
Thomas Kuhn's *The Structure of Scientific Revolutions*
Geoffrey Parker's *Global Crisis: War, Climate Change and Catastrophe in the Seventeenth Century*
Mathis Wackernagel & William Rees's *Our Ecological Footprint*

SOCIOLOGY

Michelle Alexander's *The New Jim Crow: Mass Incarceration in the Age of Colorblindness*
Gordon Allport's *The Nature of Prejudice*
Albert Bandura's *Aggression: A Social Learning Analysis*
Hanna Batatu's *The Old Social Classes And The Revolutionary Movements Of Iraq*
Ha-Joon Chang's *Kicking Away the Ladder*
W. E. B. Du Bois's *The Souls of Black Folk*
Émile Durkheim's *On Suicide*
Frantz Fanon's *Black Skin, White Masks*
Frantz Fanon's *The Wretched of the Earth*
Eric Foner's *Reconstruction: America's Unfinished Revolution, 1863-1877*
Eugene Genovese's *Roll, Jordan, Roll: The World the Slaves Made*
Jack Goldstone's *Revolution and Rebellion in the Early Modern World*
Antonio Gramsci's *The Prison Notebooks*
Richard Herrnstein & Charles A Murray's *The Bell Curve: Intelligence and Class Structure in American Life*
Eric Hoffer's *The True Believer: Thoughts on the Nature of Mass Movements*
Jane Jacobs's *The Death and Life of Great American Cities*
Robert Lucas's *Why Doesn't Capital Flow from Rich to Poor Countries?*
Jay Macleod's *Ain't No Makin' It: Aspirations and Attainment in a Low Income Neighborhood*
Elaine May's *Homeward Bound: American Families in the Cold War Era*
Douglas McGregor's *The Human Side of Enterprise*
C. Wright Mills's *The Sociological Imagination*

Thomas Piketty's *Capital in the Twenty-First Century*
Robert D. Putman's *Bowling Alone*
David Riesman's *The Lonely Crowd: A Study of the Changing American Character*
Edward Said's *Orientalism*
Joan Wallach Scott's *Gender and the Politics of History*
Theda Skocpol's *States and Social Revolutions*
Max Weber's *The Protestant Ethic and the Spirit of Capitalism*

THEOLOGY

Augustine's *Confessions*
Benedict's *Rule of St Benedict*
Gustavo Gutiérrez's *A Theology of Liberation*
Carole Hillenbrand's *The Crusades: Islamic Perspectives*
David Hume's *Dialogues Concerning Natural Religion*
Immanuel Kant's *Religion within the Boundaries of Mere Reason*
Ernst Kantorowicz's *The King's Two Bodies: A Study in Medieval Political Theology*
Søren Kierkegaard's *The Sickness Unto Death*
C. S. Lewis's *The Abolition of Man*
Saba Mahmood's *The Politics of Piety: The Islamic Revival and the Feminist Subject*
Baruch Spinoza's *Ethics*
Keith Thomas's *Religion and the Decline of Magic*

COMING SOON

Chris Argyris's *The Individual and the Organisation*
Seyla Benhabib's *The Rights of Others*
Walter Benjamin's *The Work Of Art in the Age of Mechanical Reproduction*
John Berger's *Ways of Seeing*
Pierre Bourdieu's *Outline of a Theory of Practice*
Mary Douglas's *Purity and Danger*
Roland Dworkin's *Taking Rights Seriously*
James G. March's *Exploration and Exploitation in Organisational Learning*
Ikujiro Nonaka's *A Dynamic Theory of Organizational Knowledge Creation*
Griselda Pollock's *Vision and Difference*
Amartya Sen's *Inequality Re-Examined*
Susan Sontag's *On Photography*
Yasser Tabbaa's *The Transformation of Islamic Art*
Ludwig von Mises's *Theory of Money and Credit*

The Macat Library By Discipline